WORLD WAR II

WORLD WAR II IN THE PACIFIC

by Russell Roberts

FOCUS READERS
VOYAGER

www.focusreaders.com

Copyright © 2023 by Focus Readers®, Lake Elmo, MN 55042. All rights reserved. No part of this book may be reproduced or utilized in any form or by any means without written permission from the publisher.

Focus Readers is distributed by North Star Editions:
sales@northstareditions.com | 888-417-0195

Produced for Focus Readers by Red Line Editorial.

Content Consultant: Dr. Gideon Mailer, Associate Professor of History, University of Minnesota Duluth

Photographs ©: Shutterstock Images, cover, 1, 4–5, 7, 19, 20–21, 23, 34, 40–41, 43; AP Images, 8–9, 11, 13, 45; National Photo Company Collection/Library of Congress, 14–15; U.S. Marine Corps/AP Images, 17; U.S. Navy/Library of Congress, 25; U.S. Marines/Library of Congress, 26–27; U.S. Army/Library of Congress, 29, 36; Library of Congress, 31; Joe Rosenthal/AP Images, 32–33; Galerie Bilderwelt/Hulton Archive/Getty Images, 39

Library of Congress Cataloging-in-Publication Data
Names: Roberts, Russell, 1953- author.
Title: World War II in the Pacific / by Russell Roberts.
Description: Lake Elmo, MN : Focus Readers, [2023] | Series: World War II |
    Includes index. | Audience: Grades 4-6
Identifiers: LCCN 2022007159 (print) | LCCN 2022007160 (ebook) | ISBN
    9781637392867 (hardcover) | ISBN 9781637393383 (paperback) | ISBN
    9781637394366 (pdf) | ISBN 9781637393901 (ebook)
Subjects: LCSH: World War, 1939-1945--Campaigns--Pacific Area--Juvenile
    literature. | World War, 1939-1945--Campaigns--Japan--Juvenile
    literature.
Classification: LCC D743.7 .R63 2023 (print) | LCC D743.7 (ebook) | DDC
    940.53/52--dc23/eng/20220214
LC record available at https://lccn.loc.gov/2022007159
LC ebook record available at https://lccn.loc.gov/2022007160

Printed in the United States of America
Mankato, MN
082022

ABOUT THE AUTHOR

Russell Roberts is an award-winning freelance writer who has written and published more than 100 books for both children and adults. In addition to biographies of famous people, he has written about child labor and the turning points of the US Civil War.

TABLE OF CONTENTS

CHAPTER 1
A Day of Infamy 5

CHAPTER 2
The Road to War 9

CHAPTER 3
Japan Sweeps Across the Pacific 15

CHAPTER 4
The Tide Turns 21

CHAPTER 5
Japanese Setbacks 27

A CLOSER LOOK
Pacific War Strategies 30

CHAPTER 6
On to Japan 33

A CLOSER LOOK
Life in Wartime Japan 38

CHAPTER 7
The End of the War 41

Focus on World War II in the Pacific • 46
Glossary • 47
To Learn More • 48
Index • 48

CHAPTER 1

A DAY OF INFAMY

December 7, 1941, started off quietly. It was a Sunday. For many Americans, this was a day off. They relaxed, went to church, or spent time with family and friends.

At Pearl Harbor, a US naval base on the Hawaiian island of Oahu, sailors slept late. Ships rocked gently at anchor. Unoccupied airplanes were lined up neatly in rows on airfields.

A Japanese bomber flies over the US naval base at Pearl Harbor.

Suddenly, at 7:55 a.m., dozens of Japanese planes burst out of the sky. The planes bombed ships, planes, and buildings. The attack caught the Americans completely by surprise. Screaming people desperately looked for shelter as bombs exploded around them.

The naval base had 70 warships, including 8 battleships. Torpedoes slammed into them. Japanese ships and submarines had joined the attack. US forces tried to fight back, but it was difficult with so little warning.

The attack lasted 75 minutes. In all, Japanese forces destroyed 140 US planes and damaged 80 others. Nearly 20 ships were sunk or badly damaged. More than 2,500 people were hurt or killed.

News of the attack soon blared from every radio in the United States. Many Americans were

▲ The attack on Pearl Harbor damaged all eight of the United States' battleships.

angry and stunned. Other countries were fighting in World War II (1939–1945). But the United States had not joined the war.

The next day, US President Franklin Delano Roosevelt gave a speech. He said December 7 was a day that would live in **infamy**. After his speech, Congress declared war on Japan. In response, Germany and Italy declared war on the United States. Any hopes that US troops would stay uninvolved were over.

CHAPTER 2

THE ROAD TO WAR

Since the late 1800s, Japan's military had been growing. This was part of the country's plan to modernize. It focused on building up industry and trade. In the 1850s, Japan had been isolated. But by 1900, it was an **industrial** nation that traded with many other countries. Its military had also grown strong.

During World War I (1914–1918), Japan was an ally of the United States. Japan and the United

Hideki Tojo (left) became Japan's prime minister in 1941. Before that, he led Japan's army.

States joined with several other countries. They fought against Germany, Austria-Hungary, and Turkey. After Japan's side won the war, Japan took over Germany's colonies in East Asia. As a result, Japan became the most powerful nation in the region.

An economic **depression** tore through Japan in the mid-1920s. Three million workers lost their jobs. There were street riots by people protesting the lack of jobs. Many people faced poverty. Families ate roots and tree bark to survive. These economic problems led to political upheaval. A military-dominated government took control. Its leaders began planning to invade nearby areas. They hoped to gain resources to help Japan recover.

In September 1931, Japan invaded the Chinese province of Manchuria. Japanese forces took

⚐ After the invasion of Manchuria in 1931, fighting between Japan and China continued.

over the province and renamed it Manchukuo. It became Japan's industrial center. By the late 1930s, it was producing huge amounts of cotton and steel.

The United States and other countries condemned Japan's actions in Manchuria. However, they didn't force Japan to leave the area.

Many countries were still recovering from World War I. They didn't want to start a war with Japan.

In 1937, Japan attacked China again. In response, President Roosevelt restricted trade with Japan. He knew Japan wanted US goods. He hoped the limits would get Japan to stop attacking China. But the attacks continued.

On September 1, 1939, World War II began in Europe. Germany and Italy fought against Britain, France, and other countries. In 1940, Japan joined on the side of Germany. Japan also kept taking more land in Asia. These areas included Vietnam, which was part of French Indochina at the time.

US leaders tried using **diplomacy** to stop Japan's actions. They also added trade restrictions. By October 1940, they had stopped selling oil, steel, iron, and other key resources to Japan. Japan got 80 percent of its oil from the

▲ Japanese soldiers fought against troops from the Soviet Union near the border of Manchuria in 1939.

United States. To get the oil it needed, Japan would be pressured to make a change.

Japanese leaders knew other areas in the Pacific had the resources their country needed. However, they knew seizing these areas could trigger a war with the United States. So, leaders began work on a different plan. It featured a surprise attack on Pearl Harbor.

CHAPTER 3

JAPAN SWEEPS ACROSS THE PACIFIC

Admiral Isoroku Yamamoto began planning the Pearl Harbor attack in early 1941. Yamamoto led Japan's navy. He knew Japan couldn't match the United States' industrial might. In a long war, the United States would produce far more weapons, planes, and ships. These forces could easily overwhelm Japan. For Japan to win, fighting against the United States needed to be quick and devastating.

Isoroku Yamamoto (left) was known for his excellent battle strategies.

Before 1941, World War II was centered in Europe. So far, the United States had stayed out of the conflict. However, Yamamoto believed US forces would eventually join the fight against Germany. By destroying the US fleet at Pearl Harbor, he hoped to make it impossible for the United States to fight in both Europe and the Pacific. US leaders would then be forced to negotiate peace with Japan so they could focus on fighting Germany. Japan would be able to keep the land it had taken.

The Pearl Harbor attack did cause great damage. But it wasn't the knockout blow Yamamoto wanted. Three US aircraft carriers were away from the base that day. So, they were unharmed. Six of the damaged battleships were repaired and returned to duty. In fact, the entire base was fixed and kept being used.

▲ The Philippines was a US territory. US and Filipino soldiers worked together to defend it.

Nevertheless, the next few months were very successful for Japan. Japanese forces swept across the Pacific. They quickly seized Guam and Wake Island. Japan also invaded the Philippines. This group of islands had been under US control for many years. US and Filipino troops, led by General Douglas MacArthur, tried to defend it. But Japan forced them to retreat. Japanese troops landed on Luzon, the Philippines' largest island.

They drove the US soldiers back to Luzon's west coast.

Japan also fought against British troops. Japan took over British territories such as Hong Kong and Malaya. British troops were pushed back toward Singapore. On February 15, 1942, Singapore fell to Japan. Indonesia, then called the Dutch East Indies, surrendered soon after.

The US forces in the Philippines were also pushed back. MacArthur retreated from Luzon to the tiny island of Corregidor. Finally, President Roosevelt ordered him to evacuate. MacArthur left the Philippines on March 11, 1942. But he vowed to return.

Several weeks later, the Philippines surrendered. More than 75,000 US and Filipino troops were captured. The Japanese marched the prisoners 65 miles (105 km) to prison camps.

Anyone who couldn't keep up was killed and left along the road. The five-day journey became known as the Bataan Death March. Between 3,000 and 10,000 soldiers died.

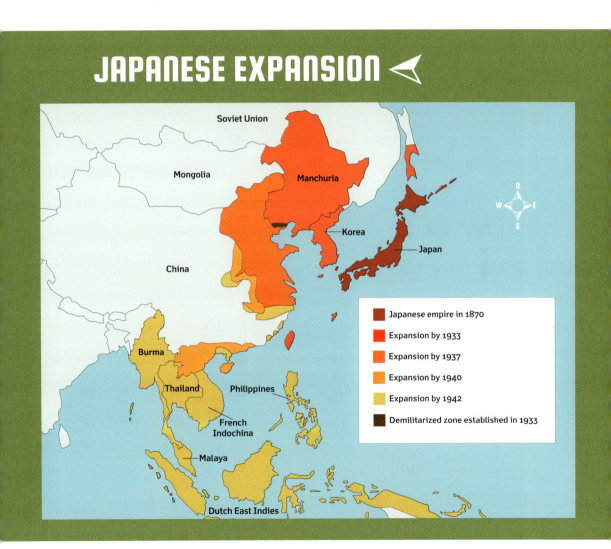

CHAPTER 4

THE TIDE TURNS

So far, Japan seemed to be winning. But the tide was about to turn. On April 18, 1942, a group of US bombers took off from an aircraft carrier in the Pacific Ocean. They flew over Tokyo and bombed the city. Each plane carried only four bombs, so the attack did little damage. But damage wasn't the main goal. The raid had shown that the Japanese weren't untouchable.

In April 1942, 16 US bombers took off from the USS *Hornet* and attacked Tokyo.

The United States and the rest of the **Allied Forces** welcomed the news. Meanwhile, the raid shocked Japan's leaders. Before, they had believed their nation was safe from attack. Now, they became determined to strengthen Japan's protective buffer. This buffer was the islands and territories around Japan that were under its control. To attack Japan, enemies would first have to fight their way through these areas. Japan's leaders wanted to make this buffer even bigger. So, they planned to invade islands near Australia.

The Allied Forces met them at the Battle of the Coral Sea in May 1942. It was the first naval battle in history in which ships from each side never saw those from the other. The fighting was done by planes launched from aircraft carriers 200 miles (322 km) apart. Each side lost several ships and many airplanes. But the battle was a

⚐ During the Battle of the Coral Sea, the USS *Lexington* exploded and sank.

strategic victory for the United States. Japan was forced to retreat. For the first time in the war, the United States had stopped a Japanese advance.

Japan's next target was the Midway Islands. This group of islands covered just 2.4 square miles (6.2 sq km). But Japan hoped to use it as a base. Midway was 1,100 miles (1,770 km) from Hawaii. From Midway, Japan could attack Pearl Harbor again.

Admiral Yamamoto planned to destroy the rest of the US Navy's Pacific Fleet at Midway. He assembled 200 ships, 700 planes, and 100,000 men. It was intended to be another surprise attack. However, the United States had broken Japan's secret naval codes. The code breakers guessed that Midway was Japan's next target. But they weren't sure. US Admiral Chester W. Nimitz gambled that the guesses were correct. He sent a large fleet of ships and submarines to Midway.

The resulting battle became the turning point of World War II in the Pacific. Over several days in early June, more than 100 US bombers swooped over Japanese ships. They sank three of Japan's aircraft carriers. Several planes refueling or rearming on the ships' decks were also destroyed. The United States lost several ships, too. But US forces stopped Japan from landing on Midway.

▲ Although the Battle of Midway was a naval battle, airplanes did most of the fighting.

The Battle of Midway was the Allied Forces' first clear victory over the Japanese navy. Japan lost huge numbers of ships, planes, and pilots. Its navy was no longer capable of launching invasions or large-scale attacks. The United States and its allies could start their own **offensive** operations. They began plans to invade islands Japan had captured.

CHAPTER 5

JAPANESE SETBACKS

On August 7, 1942, US forces landed on three of the Solomon Islands. These islands were Guadalcanal, Florida, and Tulagi. Each had been taken over by Japan. This was the first US attack in World War II to involve both land and sea operations.

By August 9, Florida and Tulagi were in US hands. However, the fight for Guadalcanal took months. Allied troops would appear to gain an

Fierce fighting took place on Guadalcanal, which was the site of an important airfield.

advantage. Then Japan would resupply its forces at night and be ready to fight again the next day.

By February 1943, Japan had lost 680 aircraft, 24 warships, and 30,000 soldiers. These losses were so great that Japan abandoned Guadalcanal. The United States lost 29 ships and 615 aircraft. Approximately 7,100 US soldiers were killed.

Japan faced more setbacks in New Guinea. Japanese soldiers first landed there in January 1942. But moving across New Guinea was slow and dangerous work. Dense forests, high mountains, and razor-sharp grasses covered the island. Soldiers also faced flooding, mudslides, insects, and wild animals. **Militia** and volunteers from Australia and New Guinea blocked Japanese advances for a year until US troops could arrive.

By the beginning of 1943, the southeastern end of New Guinea was cleared of Japanese soldiers.

⚠ The US Air Force bombed a Japanese port at Hansa Bay, New Guinea.

The threat to Australia ceased. Even so, fighting in New Guinea continued until the end of the war. More than 200,000 Japanese soldiers died.

In April 1943, Japan suffered another blow. Admiral Yamamoto was killed. Allied code breakers had learned his travel plans. They planned an attack to shoot down his plane. The war was swiftly turning against Japan.

A CLOSER LOOK

PACIFIC WAR STRATEGIES

In 1943, US troops began using a strategy known as island-hopping. They left heavily defended islands alone. Instead, they attacked islands that were less protected. US troops then blockaded the bypassed islands. They stopped reinforcements and supplies from reaching the bypassed islands. The Japanese defenders were cut off. They were left to surrender or starve.

This strategy gave US troops an advantage. But they still had to move through tough jungle terrain. They also faced fierce Japanese fighters.

Japanese soldiers often followed the Bushido code. This code said it was better to die in battle than to be taken prisoner. So, some Japanese soldiers chose to fight to the death. The Battle of Tarawa was an example. On November 20, 1943,

▲ US soldiers wade through deep mud on Bougainville. This island is near New Guinea.

US Marines invaded Tarawa. This small atoll in the Gilbert Islands was defended by 4,500 Japanese troops. The soldiers dug trenches and set up a series of other defenses.

Bitter fighting raged for four days. At the end of the battle, many Japanese soldiers repeatedly charged. The soldiers knew they would probably lose. But they tried to kill as many US soldiers as possible. This tactic was known as a banzai attack. Only 17 Japanese soldiers survived.

CHAPTER 6

ON TO JAPAN

As the months progressed, the Allies fought their way through the Pacific islands. Troops led by US Admiral William F. Halsey moved north through the Solomon Islands. General MacArthur's forces advanced along New Guinea's northern coast.

Meanwhile, Nimitz led an invasion in the central Pacific. His troops fought in the Gilbert and Marshall Islands. By early 1944, each force

A famous photograph shows US soldiers raising the US flag during the Battle of Iwo Jima.

had advanced. With each victory, US troops moved closer to being able to invade Japan.

On June 15, 1944, Allied troops attacked Saipan in the Mariana Islands. On July 7, facing certain defeat, thousands of Japanese soldiers

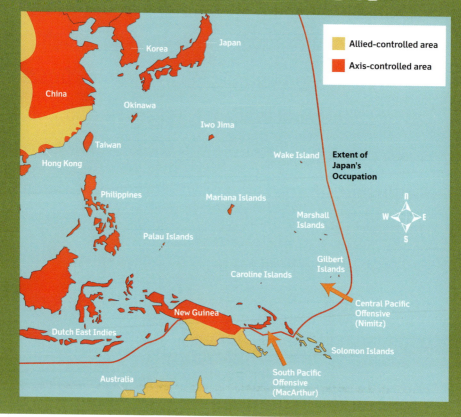

POSITIONS IN NOVEMBER 1943

and civilians staged a banzai attack. It lasted 12 hours. By the end, more than 4,300 Japanese soldiers had died.

Fighting reached the Philippines by early August. On October 20, US troops landed on Leyte Island. General Douglas MacArthur waded ashore. As promised, he had returned to the Philippines.

The Battle of Leyte Gulf lasted from October 23 to October 26. It was the largest naval battle in history. It involved 200,000 men and 282 ships. And it took place over 100,000 square miles (259,000 sq km) of water. The Japanese fleet was badly beaten.

During the battle, Japan introduced a new weapon. Pilots packed aircraft with explosives. Then, they purposely crashed into Allied ships. They tried to cause as much damage as possible.

▲ US soldiers fight in the Philippines in April 1945.

They also died in the process. These pilots were known as kamikazes.

On land, the Japanese gave up ground inch by inch. Fighting was especially fierce in Manila, the Philippines' capital city. By March 1945, people could see from one end of the city to the other. Nothing remained standing to block the view.

The Allies' next target was Iwo Jima. This island was halfway between the Mariana Islands and Japan. It could act as a base where airplanes could refuel. US soldiers invaded Iwo Jima on

February 19, 1945. For 36 days, approximately 21,000 Japanese defenders fought bitterly. Finally, on March 26, the fighting ended. Only 216 Japanese soldiers survived.

US forces invaded Okinawa on April 1, 1945. This island was just 360 miles (579 km) from the Japanese mainland. Its 130,000 defenders fought desperately. They knew that if Okinawa fell, Japan was next. At sea, kamikaze planes rained down on US ships.

The battle ended on June 22. The United States suffered 49,000 casualties. But it won the fight. The way to Japan was now open.

CONSIDER THIS ◁

Can you think of other battles where armies suffered great losses but won strategic victories?

A CLOSER LOOK

LIFE IN WARTIME JAPAN

Life in wartime Japan was difficult. As men left to serve in the military, women and children took over their jobs. They worked in mines, in factories, and on farms. Many worked long hours.

Shortages of everyday items became common. Stores ran out of socks, toilet paper, buttons, and matches. Doctors and medicine were also hard to find.

One of the worst shortages was food. People waited in line for hours to get a tiny bit of food. Desperate for anything to eat, people ate ground-up acorns or cooked grubs. Some ate stray dogs and cats.

Some people got food illegally on the black market. They paid extremely high prices. And if caught, people could be arrested.

▲ Allied air raids destroyed many homes and buildings in cities throughout Japan.

In addition, Japan's government demanded total loyalty from people of all ages. Military police groups watched and listened for signs of disloyalty. Anyone suspected of being disloyal could be arrested and tortured.

The government controlled the newspapers, too. Papers mainly printed stories of heroic Japanese soldiers. Defeats like Midway were reported as victories. Writers who wrote anything unfavorable lost their jobs or were imprisoned.

CHAPTER 7

THE END OF THE WAR

The future looked grim as the US military prepared to invade Japan. Experts thought the war would last at least three more years. They predicted one million casualties. US forces would have to fight two million enemy soldiers. Japanese civilians would likely fight them, too.

The war in Europe had already ended. Germany had surrendered on May 7, 1945. So, the US military focused on Japan. US planes had been

B-29 bombers rained bombs on Japan, setting fire to large areas.

firebombing Japan. They dropped bombs filled with napalm on Japanese cities. The bombs caused huge fires that spread quickly. One attack in March 1945 destroyed 15 square miles (39 sq km) of Tokyo. It killed more than 100,000 people. Still, Japan did not surrender.

However, the United States had an even more powerful weapon. Back in 1942, President Roosevelt had approved the Manhattan Project. Hundreds of scientists worked to create an **atomic bomb**. In July 1945, they successfully tested one. By this time, Roosevelt had died. He had a stroke on April 12, 1945. Harry S. Truman replaced him as president. Truman decided to use an atomic bomb against Japan. He hoped to bring the war to a quicker end.

On August 6, 1945, a US plane dropped one atomic bomb on the city of Hiroshima.

▲ The atomic bomb destroyed 70 percent of the buildings in Hiroshima, Japan.

The explosion created a flash 10 times as bright as the sun. The blast was also extremely hot. Temperatures reached thousands of degrees. Bronze statues melted. Fire and smoke engulfed the city, and 80,000 people died instantly.

The United States demanded unconditional surrender from Japan. But Emperor Hirohito didn't respond. So, Truman approved the use of a second bomb. This one hit the city of Nagasaki on August 9. It killed more than 73,000 people and injured nearly 75,000 others.

43

Hirohito now knew Japan must surrender. On August 15, 1945, he gave a speech on the radio announcing the war's end.

Japan's formal surrender took place on September 2, 1945. The ceremony was held on a ship in Tokyo Bay. President Truman chose Douglas MacArthur to accept Japan's surrender. Representatives from Japan's government signed the surrender documents. General MacArthur signed next, followed by representatives from other Allied countries.

World War II was officially over. But Allied forces remained in Japan. MacArthur was named the Supreme Commander for the Allied Powers. He was put in charge of **occupied** Japan. The country had been devastated. Half of its cities lay in ruins. One-third of its industries had been destroyed. And its population was near starvation.

▲ Japan's foreign minister, Mamoru Shigemitsu, signs the surrender documents.

MacArthur worked with Japanese leaders to make changes. He helped draft a new constitution and set up elections. The US occupation of Japan ended in 1952. But the effects of the war would be felt long afterward.

CONSIDER THIS ◁

Do you think it was right for the United States to occupy Japan after the war? Why or why not?

FOCUS ON

WORLD WAR II IN THE PACIFIC

Write your answers on a separate piece of paper.

1. Write a paragraph describing Japan's goals in attacking Pearl Harbor.

2. Do you think President Truman made the right decision to drop atomic bombs on Japan? Why or why not?

3. Which type of attack involved airplanes packed with explosives purposely crashing into ships?

>   **A.** kamikaze
>   **B.** banzai
>   **C.** island-hopping

4. Why did Japan want to strengthen its protective buffer after the April 1942 attack on Tokyo?

>   **A.** The attack proved that no one could invade Japan.
>   **B.** The attack made an invasion of Japan seem more likely.
>   **C.** The attack made an invasion of Japan seem less likely.

Answer key on page 48.

GLOSSARY

Allied Forces
The victorious countries of World War II, including Britain, France, the Soviet Union, and the United States.

atomic bomb
A powerful weapon that creates an explosion by splitting atoms.

depression
A period of time when an area's economy struggles, prices rise, and people lose their jobs.

diplomacy
The process of solving problems or influencing countries' actions by talking and making agreements.

industrial
Producing many goods in factories.

infamy
Being famous for a bad or evil action.

militia
A group of citizens trained to carry out military actions, usually during times of emergency.

occupied
Under the control of a foreign country or invading army.

offensive
Involving attacks made by a military to gain territory or take control of a target.

strategic victory
When the results of a battle damage the enemy's long-term ability to continue fighting a war.

TO LEARN MORE

BOOKS

Carser, A. R. *The US Decision to Drop the Atomic Bomb*. Minneapolis: Abdo Publishing, 2021.

Miles, John C. *Fighting Forces of World War II at Sea*. North Mankato, MN: Capstone Press, 2020.

Taylor, Diane C. *World War II: From the Rise of the Nazi Party to the Dropping of the Atomic Bomb*. White River Junction, VT: Nomad Press, 2018.

NOTE TO EDUCATORS

Visit **www.focusreaders.com** to find lesson plans, activities, links, and other resources related to this title.

INDEX

atomic bombs, 42–43

Gilbert Islands, 31, 33–34

Iwo Jima, 34, 36

kamikazes, 35–37

MacArthur, Douglas, 17–18, 33–35, 44–45

Manchuria, 10–11, 19

Midway Islands, 23–25, 39

New Guinea, 28–29, 33–34

Nimitz, Chester W., 24, 33–34

occupied Japan, 44–45

Okinawa, 37

Pearl Harbor, 5–6, 13, 15–16, 23

Philippines, 17–19, 34–36

Roosevelt, Franklin Delano, 7, 12, 18, 42

Solomon Islands, 27, 33–34

Truman, Harry S., 42–44

Yamamoto, Isoroku, 15–16, 24, 29

Answer Key: 1. Answers will vary; **2.** Answers will vary; **3.** A; **4.** B